I0843429

FRENEMY TRAITOR

GLOBALISLAM

written and illustrated by

Karen Kellock Ph.D.

Manual for Superior Men

This is a complete theory based on Einstein physics, Political Psychology, Systems Theory and Archetypal Psychiatry.

FORMULA

**All success attraction
All disease obstruction
All recovery elimination**

You must fast on all three

OBSTRUCTIONS:

**People
Habit
Food**

FRENEMY TRAITOR

The self-downputting comes from marching to a different reality/being misunderstood constantly.   Those who conform/get along with pack, tribe or klatch don't feel like this seeing self as a lost case. Eventually they'll put genius in a class all his own but in the meantime life is hell if weak/not bold. Take your time, do it right. You'll spring up as savior in your field and all will know your name, aye. You swam in muddy waters like in California so you took for granted sin's ok but it's God you betrayed. But no matter what you did under social hypnotism it'll all be ok just repent and start fresh today.

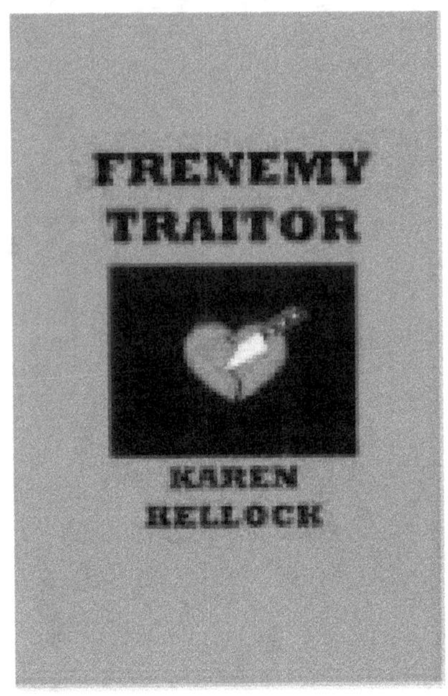

Preface to FRENEMY TRAITORS

FRENEMY TRAITORS

SAINTS HAVE STINGING CONSCIENCE

The saints have a stinging conscience and that's why you feel like this not from despicability sis.

You're stuck in the Nigredo stage of making gold: "no one's as bad as me"-- knowing this consoles.

Gradually this feeling of badness takes it's rightful place and your good points arise/illuminate.

I take in homeless animals, I love my friends and family, I keep immaculate house and I get up early.

You are rebuilding necessary self-love to proceed as a queen tho' a dove. They call it velvet glove.

The self-downputting comes from marching to a different reality/being misunderstood constantly.

Those who conform/get along with pack, tribe or klatch don't feel like this seeing self as a lost case.

CONFORMISTS DON'T FEEL IT

The warm fuzzy feelings of belonging veil feelings of self guilt, shame or embarrassment for living.

Eventually they'll put genius in a class all his own but in the meantime life is hell if weak/not bold.

Take your time, do it right. You'll spring up as savior in your field and all will know your name, aye.

FRENEMY TRAITOR

You swam in muddy waters like in California so you took for granted sin's ok but it's God you betrayed.

But no matter what you did under social hypnotism it'll all be ok just repent and start fresh today.

BETRAYALS IN SIN

If in sin people betray you all around and eventually your best friend will tire and give up, confounded.

People are cruel so find one that loves you and build on that: with boundaries, wall and locked gate.

Wolfpacks kill deviants who starve outside the pack. This is the hero's journey and comeback.

If you won't or can't conform you'll be all alone and this will be a rocky road that ends in pure gold.

Envision yourself in a big balloon having cut off obstruction so you're rising above the problem.

Endure for a while longer as the conversion takes place and a whole new vista opens/sins erased.

Like a giant jigsaw puzzle snapping together perfectly all pieces of your life will make sense finally.

The things you went thru when younger were awful but you thought you had to so just got thru it.

CRINGED ACCEPTANCE

When you cringingly accept things going against spirit the results are devastating/later PTSD.

I am seven again, like before this whole black cloud began. It's safe here, like having a good friend.

FRENEMY TRAITOR

Trauma brings on moral collapse then the hedge of protection is down as evil flows on in.

You witnessed it, you lived it. Now you're whole again, you've overcome it and built back up.

I had such a stinging conscience and was so sensitive I couldn't be around anyone for too long.

You're so different you're a revolution/legend onto yourself and now attract satellites/disciples.

If you give up your dreams/truckle back in your life will be rocky/frustrating as a has-been.

I couldn't give up my vision and identity was totally tied to my work. To stop was soul suicide girl.

Seeing how much of life was taken up by mental illness you're grateful to Jesus who died for this.

People get sick physically but also mentally. In weird/unsafe environments its the only way.

FORGIVE FOR GOD'S VENGEANCE

Forgive foe with grace, forgiveness, mercy and love and you're free: God goes on a killing spree.

A main marker of dependency is advice-seeking of the enemy, a narcissist putting you in jeopardy.

With knowledge of how they screwed you up it's easier to let em all go and then progress on up.

When a culture coarsens, degrades or becomes noise to our ears the saints and genius all disappear.

Embarrassment over faux pas or mistakes lessens when you see it's the collective subconscious.

FRENEMY TRAITOR

FRENEMIES IN THE FAMILY

When your own mother is the biggest calumnious gossiper it's a helluva thing to accept sir.

When your own sisters blabbed your weaknesses everywhere it's hard to forgive the girls.

When it was your mother wrecking every new relationship and deliberately bringing ruin, heck!

This is about: spiritual decline, psychos and women killing children and civilization going into ruin.

Home was an unstable, unsupportive atmosphere with parents on drugs/alcohol: triggers, fear.

Cause of emotional illness: was home an unstable, vacillating atmosphere of constant fuss?

Your brain was wired for a grenade range of paybacks and hypervigilance, that's why you're like this.

BRAIN IN DECLINE

Just when things are running smoothly and there is tranquility she causes eruption like a bee.

The brain of the peace-breaker is wired to the prior, a grenade range of hope/identity-destroyers.

My brain went from ignoring/not hearing insults to getting pretty pissed about it or I'd sulk.

You couldn't care less once you got your audacity back cuz adapting to Elmer Fudd was so sad.

If you can hear inner voices yelling at you it's cuz the dam witches *were* yelling/it's like a photo.

FRENEMY TRAITOR

They're in hell suckin' up the flames. After being their victim you should never think of em again.

GOD REMOVES BLACK CLOUD

I relocated. Suddenly free of all detractors, gossipers, calumnious enviers and minimizers I'm elated.

God's people will NOT be condemned: He removes the black cloud of past sins/present reflections.

Alcohol's a conduit to the devil, clear and simple. Even if it's just your ego it can cause trouble.

I too get depressed over the past: why didn't I say this or that but does it not always bring distress?

You spend half of your life screwing up and the second half remorsing over it: to hell with this.

When I finally grew up a new vista opened up and I was 7 again before a black cloud mixed it up.

You must have an indomitable spirit that recidivates: bounces back up after a drought or spats.

s there wrath amongst you? Then there is SIN: a bad habit, association or where you've been.

LET GOD BE YOUR SOUL TIE

If you've already given God your soul & mind it's no big thing if a relationship has dropped aside.

People overestimate how much others notice their mistakes but it feels like they all do ok.

People are too consumed with their problems to dwell on yours tho' they'll needle you of course.

FRENEMY TRAITOR

Talking terrible to husband was characteristic of the wife of the alcoholic syndrome/contagion.

I've been thrown to the wolves so I know what that feels like: an open prison cuz your hedge is down.

No boundaries allowed, you're just thrown out there with em. No privacy, personal control or fun.

HAUNTED HOUSE INSIDE

Suddenly I was afraid of his haunted house inside. Serial false identities and a bloated "I".

A small liberal town is an open society and that means you have no privacy. I left and am now free.

A queen knows who she is/her value, an average woman is mocked down by the world and made blue.

For the average it's according to what the world dictates and then marching to her low minded fate.

Queens avoid soul tie entanglements--the pit of all confusion and emotional disorder like sex.

QUEENS ALIGN WITH GOD'S PLAN

She is aligned with the Creator's plan for her, transcending all expectations on lower tiers.

By avoiding lowminds everything in her life comes into order around the Creators plan: the divine.

When God brings her into emotional order she natural accepts or rejects the elements around her.

Does this new thing align with who she is, or does it not align? There's no other question: yes/no, aye.

FRENEMY TRAITOR

If she's queen conscious in the way she thinks then things immediately sting and she reacts.

It was a horrible time in chemical hades. They'd put me on SRIs--the insane effects lasted decades.

YOUR REACTIONS INDICATE YOU

It's what she reacts to or doesn't react to defining her consciousness and everyone knows it.

They put most popular teacher on SRIs and suddenly everyone hated her, feeling duped sir.

I became a collapsed vessel overnight, unable to stand against the narrative-- the liberal onslaught.

God'll get em for murdering your rep and soul too. Calumny is a sin and besides no longer true.

MY PH.D. IN THE STREETS

It was all a big black tunnel I had to endure and overcome, my Ph.D. in the Streets, ugh.

If you're with Christ the world comes against you now. Satan rules by releasing a legion of demons.

There is no lukewarm so the devil in them hates the Christ in you: it's principalities/powers Sue.

The liberal desert town was an open society and no one had any privacy. No one had any fences see.

That's where I learned this about human nature--by being imposed on, to object made me a hater.

I hated it as I lost my own reality in the hodgepodge but didn't know enough to be boundaried/tough.

FRENEMY TRAITOR

Once a woman sees she wears the crown her life shifts into divine alignment and it all prospers.

What steers queens around soul tie entanglements? When they wanna leave, she lets them.

If he wants to leave a queen lets him go. Cuz he's either a clown or plain stupid, that's all she knows.

REJECTION IS A GIANT BLESSING

The greatest thing is certain people leaving your life who you thought you couldn't live without.

With time we see it really wasn't about their rejection but our Father's protection: careful ma'am.

Average women beg them to stay but Queens let em go: they stay outa soul ties bringing them low.

Queens avoid soul ties because they do NOT pursue men--they trust God to bring the right one in.

They're involved in the world around em but never chase, thus soul ties are avoided/erased.

Every time a woman chases [or lurks on his pages] she loses precious self-esteem: it's inevitable see.

WATCH WHAT YOU ATTEND TO

If a queen chases a clown she's never around when a king is pursuing her: it's a pie of divided attention.

If a woman chases a man she's never in a position to be found. What is being rejected is God's plan.

The queen won't chase you cuz while she's doing that the right one can't find her/it's unfortunate.

FRENEMY TRAITOR

A king will never identify his wife if she's chasing another man so sit tight ad pray for God's plan.

A woman chasing a man becomes increasingly more desperate and it's sickening to him you twit.

Even lurking on his pages drains her self-esteem like water shaking from a bucket, just forget it.

As self-esteem drains out her self value becomes attached to her age, size or money in the bank.

While the average are chasing with soul ties queens maximize their lives as individuals, aye.

As she maximizes her virtue her husband rises up to recognize his wife and approve of her too.

God would never send a man into her life she'd have to chase. Just the thought is so degrading ok.

He who findeth a wife finds a good thing and obtains favor of the Lord--he is not landed by her.

WRONG FOCUS CUTS OUT KINGS

The prospective wife must be available and if she's chasing a clown she falls too far below.

A queen won't stop chasing until she knows what she brings to the table, not a cheap sale.

She stops chasing when she realizes the reward is a man's favor. He adores and is proud of her.

The favor a wife brings to her husband is unbelievable, soaring, profitable and God ordained it all.

High frequency women do not respond to low frequency men. Flattery won't work if he's a low mind.

FRENEMY TRAITOR

They discern low energy and don't respond to it: no entanglements with dead logs or twits.

Low frequency men make a woman feel sexualized but never seen. This is despicably unqueenly.

Such men fertilize her insecurities but never elevate her self-perspective--her complaints are rejected.

They fertilize her insecurities in bed but then these all grow to explosive proportions instead.

Being hidden her self-esteem is trashed': he mates with her in the bushes but ignores her in town.

Men who trigger her but never secure her show flip flops from emotions/tears to another lure.

LOW FREQUENCY MEN CAUSE TRAUMA

Low frequency men simply compound her trauma but say they wanna help like her lost poppa.

These low men compound trauma and prevent a sense of safety, I was scared to death suddenly.

They do not bring any sense of respect or honor. You feel enslaved soon to such manipulators.

A queen is nice to all but will never entertain a man on this low frequency, it's always an insult see.

Low frequency men value stats like age, money, beauty, SMV but God's man sees far deeper reality.

"Can I bring you out mama?" Oh no no no, bless you but I have so many things going on now.

She doesn't give her time/attention to it or get caught up for in this era few can appreciate the rare.

FRENEMY TRAITOR

Boys ask her out, she isn't interested, they are offended and turn on the pressure, she calls sheriff.

Amos 3: 3 says "Can two walk together except they agree?" Others impose lowness on a queen.

A woman is constantly brought down as men project lowness on her. She must confront or go under.

THE QUEEN IS CAPPED EARLY

A queen is constantly undercut/overridden. She must boldly take her throne but it's forbidden.

You tell your own intelligence and spiritual discernment by the person you've attached yourself to.

Unless you wanna be invaded by his buddies you gotta tell him to stay away, that's how it is today.

A lowminded guy brings all his buddies to her house but a queen cannot take this, it is ridiculous.

He can't stand tranquility so when things are relaxed he creates trouble out of things that don't exist.

Oh God such bad memories and definitely not the life for me. I want to be truly free/not treachery.

HER FREQUENCY NEEDS ELEVATION

Serial attachments to lowminds shows her own frequency needed elevation [which it is now].

If she doesn't shift into high frequency she can't discern the radio waves she's to tune into see.

No matter how many kings God sends her way she can't locate them nor they her: not tuned in.

FRENEMY TRAITOR

She must say: I've been living at a lower frequency than I deserve & let low men into my life for sure.

Thou shall not plow with ass and ox together, don't even give a place to the devil, be alone until.

Yokes are only safe with two beasts on same level, two unlikes will hurt each other like the devil.

UNSAFE YOKES

Same stature, temperament and similar goals: otherwise doesn't matter how fine he is girl.

They avoid soul tie entanglements by letting em leave, never pursuing nor responding to lowness.

Queens respect their intuition/inner discernment. The biggest red flag is a spirit in disagreement.

If her spirit's uneasy about somebody it's the biggest warning of life see and she heeds it instantly.

Soul ties occur when priorities are out of alignment. It should be God, me and others not men first.

IDEALIZE GOD NOT MAN

She's pushed God so far to the side and idolized the man instead that she's warped/minimized.

If she prioritizes God He teaches her how to prioritize or love herself--by what she evades from hell.

Putting God first means she's never looking to a man to invalidate or give her a sense of worth.

God gives her self-love and out of that she's able to determine how to love others, from above.

FRENEMY TRAITOR

If she loves God with all her heart, soul and mind it means no entry points for those soul ties.

That woman already has a soul tie with God and He has it on lock--no entry points for Elmer Fudd.

I thank God He showed me who he really was--the guy I was mesmerized with despite his gross talk.

A JEALOUS GOD LOCKS DOWN

That's what God does, as our earthly father should have: give us the scoop on a bad man.

To be locked down by jealous God is so comforting, like a real earthly father should've always been.

God is jealous and doesn't want men's paws all over his daughter and He'll even take em out I swear.

There's no relationship ending that she can't survive after giving God her heart/soul/mind.

They avoid soul ties by choosing relationships based NOT on what they want but don't want.

STATS OR DEEP THOUGHTS

Not his height or wealth but he doesn't drink or smoke, he's faithful, loyal and very reliable folks.

She's had the mediocre, weak or joyless other and knows exactly what she wants in a feller.

You get what you want and end up with what you don't want so it's more important to go against.

You get what you want and end up with what you don't want cuz it blinds your eyes to the obvious.

FRENEMY TRAITOR

Choosing what you want is type over character, what you don't want is something far deeper.

That's why queens ask questions to reveal character, to be certain it's not what I don't want sir.

I don't want to go for something appealing to me and end up with something lethal FOR me.

Miss average gets her tall handsome man but then he abuses her later cuz she didn't vet for that.

Queens close their sexual gates and that's how they avoid soul tie entanglements/bad fate.

Queens never run rabid sexually esp. in eras of debauchery. They close gates and choose wisely.

An insecure woman seeks security in sex though it's just a glance that's soon rejected/passed.

If she does have sex partners they aren't clowns but kings and even that's too much info see.

Queens close up sir: they don't play with sex nor allow men to sample them as in hookup culture.

The biggest mistake a woman can make is to give a man her body thinking he'll return his heart ok.

As women we swam in muddy waters/made many mistakes but it doesn't mean we're worthless.

PEACE AND REST

God brings you to queenliness where you belong to finally demand what you deserved all along.

I pray soul tie entanglements are broken off your life--every man you can't get out of spirit or mind.

FRENEMY TRAITOR

That man your body's addicted to: it instantly reverses when the soul tie disperses/is removed.

As every yoke in life is broken/destroyed it's the essence of freedom from danger/annoyance.

Freedom, peace and rest: after a life of one painful soul tie after another of bondage and distress.

A soul tie is a nasty spirit, you should learn of it then avoid it. A haunted house inside: forget it.

WOMEN USE SMEAR CAMPAIGNS

When a woman's weapons are smear campaigns she's right in line with the rest of the female race.

I cringed from smear campaigns since age five. False accusation was what I endured all my life.

Not smart enough to know me they'd catch me in bad webs of common man's understanding see.

The nasty false accusations of two older sisters she had to live with as all took their word on it.

Taking the herd or group's view on something rather than one's own is just social psychology son.

People hear falsehoods and tuck em away as true. This is human nature from the beginning, whew.

Being beaten up by world was the best thing to happen to this girl cuz from mom it wasn't learned.

She may have said it but I didn't learn it--I swam in muddy waters and sin was taken for granted.

Now an established belle I sit behind my locked gate, the most important thing in life I'd say.

FRENEMY TRAITOR

My answer was to stay alone, don't expect too much, don't get involved cuz they'll throw a punch.

I may make mistakes but I wrote em so I'll trust that. Eat right, repent, forgive, write--that's that.

Is it anxiety and panic or ELATION when I get so high I can't stand it? Racing heart: I pray about it.

Young love is about passion, old love is about accommodation and that's happiness son.

HIX POLITIX

Higher crime, exploding borders and high inflation--then killing children as a culture is unravelling.

The angel of death and brutality rules Mexico now. People are killed in prison dungeons, wow.

As a culture goes into judgement and ruin you see dark Satanic things like the killing of children.

Those of us who would NEVER attack anyone unless they attack us need to be armed sis.

There's 3 x more homicides in Mexico than here yet no one can own a gun there--it goes together.

Principalities and powers have now made their move releasing their sleeper cells of Satanists.

What we need in crisis is armed good guys, not Joe Biden taking our means of self-defense, aye.

Gun laws don't work. Look at New York, Chicago & California: No guns but more violence sir.

A psycho goes on killing spree and they take revenge on you and me/rights to defend ourselves see.

FRENEMY TRAITOR

Psychos and women killing children: this marks the end of civilization to the dark anarchy of Satan.

GREAT ARTISTS IN HISTORY

Great artists had great output despite wars and depressions. We gotta work/self expressions.

Understatement and supreme subtlety is my way and if you don't get it that's ok just go away.

Brick by brick I built an empire, an electronic Taj Mahal: each detail important/nothing too trivial.

Promotion is not about bragging about the great "I" but doing a Great Work and letting them decide.

Constant anxiety: what is the answer? Turn off news [repeat/filler] and just be a headline reader.

The proverbs are what you call "essentially true" and that's why they may ring a bell with you.

I get my identity from what I create and DO not from self-promotion and a buncha selfies too.

FRENEMY TRAITOR

Above all block all time wasters. Now you're in charge--with people you must manage him/her.

Once you get into the right brain (cornucopia) stay there by refusing to be tracked anymore!

Even these news videos are a waste of time. Too circuitous/repetitive, just read headlines.

It's just temporal reality--let's go to eternity shall we? That was Einstein's major interest, truly.

Let your mind go with free rein. Don't let anything track it again cuz life is a pie, recall that saying.

No tunnel-vision: Stay in the right brain and when right time comes you'll move into happy action.

It's Holy Spirit Ease. The key to work is to WAIT cuz it's your creative spirit, destiny/fate.

I'm not gonna start till I hear that click in my head. Paul Newman

Keep shaking loose previous concepts. Switch to music, take a walk, become simpler--it works.

Genius is characterized by the capacity for leisure, would-be genius has incapacity (he only works).

Retirement is like taking off a straightjacket and putting on some cozy pajamas: ah, at last.

Anyone who does not believe in miracles is not a realist. Audrey Hepburn

FRENEMY TRAITOR

Grandstanding: Making videos about a tragic event and making it all about you instead.

After forgiveness everything falls into perfect place. You don't elect or plan just carried away.

Can't have fear and faith and those without faith can't please God so give up fear and be strong.

If you don't like it don't come here that's how it works.

Don't drink with work buddies cuz if they're trying to impress boss they'll throw you under the buss.

The deep/sagacious prefer old movies, why is that? No sex, boobs or tech effects (a hex).

Wretched behavior is when God gives us up to our desires/sins (and the compulsions therein).

Sometimes I get weak and the past is my guide.

Eat, sleep, write.

You are made so batty/crazy keeping people away but I thought you said you wanted fame?

Guests: they burrow in then can't get rid of em. Like fish after 3 days they smell, just sayin'.

The more hands on deck doesn't make it more efficient, more often they're a burden darn it.

Why can't we trust anyone? Due to the total depravity of man until he's saved and begins again.

FRENEMY TRAITOR

To skillfully manage human relations you first gotta know about em and that's my reason for livin'.

To be a writer gotta go thru the ringer first: squashed and burned then of humans you've learned.

I don't know why God chose me to be a vessel for a Creative Act but it's a real miracle in fact.

If you're a writer you write and if a painter you paint. Stop saying what you are if in reality you ain't.

Don't give em the time of day, the dumb. They know nothing and waste your energy. Walk away, gently.

You've got to stop work to "take distance". Get away from it, see it differently, RELAX.

You gotta choose sides. You can't have both worlds cuz God's wrath on you will fall on me.

They're either family or not. We're down to basics and God said our enemies are in the house.

Everyone wants something and you gotta be shrewd to save yourself from a disaster happening.

Is there anyone out there who understands, anyone? You all seem half asleep and unconcerned.

Put cat doors everywhere. They have their own underworld--enable and appreciate it, share.

Life is a wonderful opportunity to let God come thru thee in a Creative Act making them free to be.

FRENEMY TRAITOR

Take a *mental* vacation for where to escape? Your home is a palace and outside it's dangerous.

Wild animals have become nocturnal to avoid humans and I've done that too to be a good student.

Ph.D. in Streets: Depths of hell seeing horrible things and people so now that you know, be sweet.

The most productive time possible is through productive puttering or just looking out the window.

If you have pets you gotta clean up after them. Establish routines then life is happy and fun.

I just wanna think without any interruptions whatsoever. Cats/dogs are bad enough, whatever.

Time to stop/look at the wind thru the trees and that'll shake everything loose so you can see.

Art is to edify not to disgust/make us wanna die.

It's not I, God has gifted me but not for free.

We are made in the image of God so all they do is degrade that image--don't degrade if yourself.

They're already reprobate if can't see God in the heavens. An orchid, a star and they're doubtin'.

Don't worry about it--be on vacation, always. That is the right brain like a child on Saturdays.

FRENEMY TRAITOR

The reason people don't answer emails is they just don't want to/they've got too much to do.

Real men and real women are always right cuz they're guided by what is right and SEE what's right.

It's old fashioned to do what's right and not do what's wrong, it's whatever works in the throng.

All angry people are prideful and can't know God for pride is the nature of Satan. Jesse Lee Peterson

The wicked never question what they want to do, the righteous are restrained/humble too.

Angry people can't love cuz anger is the nature of Satan and his destruction.

I understand it but can't live with it. Admit to yourself you're playing God and wrong.

Forgiveness is the most important since it's disburdening you of a lifetime of distorted implants.

An entire lifetime you've been carrying this around. Forgiveness is success/new dawn.

Forgive only after repentance or create criminals.

Think of how long you've carried this burden then see the power and efficiency of forgiveness.

Forgive them (know not what they do) so God forgives you (released for success in all you do).

FRENEMY TRAITOR

 **I forgive you totally but can't live with ya, Nutty.**

The strong have internal strength (it's called restraint) while the weak man gives in to everything.

It hurts letting people go but recall why you did it: moral ineptitude like it's bred right into it.

Ego is blind. It can't see how transparent it is in a bind and it's embarrassing to those with a mind.

Kept forgiving her greedy overreach each time more, then of great danger I became aware.

Marriage manual by KK: End every sentence with "honey" and talk to him like a little baby boy.

Just sitting and thinking is working so don't let em ever say you're not accomplishing anything.

No mercy without justice. Forgiveness not a free pass to repeat, must turn from wrongs you idiot.

Parents: Whatever you are the kids become. You can't hide the fornication it's a spiritual thing.

Stringent order (they hate that) makes me so happy and puritanical order began our culture.

Leave the path open don't plan a thing. Zero, vacuity, open: that's the highest way of thinking.

Protect yourself cuz whenever they get the upper hand they'll take all your stuff.

FRENEMY TRAITOR

Be still and know God. Your over-reaction to the problem is the whole problem so stay calm.

It's amazing how a tiny thing in the environment can wreck your life and reality in a minute.

Just think, you never have to go thru this again.

Overcome anger then see what's going on.

You've got to tell the truth because we're fighting against evil.

Like shit on the shoe or fish after three days they just won't go away: you must insist or die.

The righteous man is delivered from trouble, in his place the wicked man goes in as a ransom. Prov. 21

Oh the feeling of going beyond a person/problem! Like a cornucopic paradise of bliss opens.

Most important part of house: locked gate, wall/fence.

Path out of insanity is unique. You must unpeel distorted implants that put you up a creek.

The maid did it. She had a demon in her and we went insane adapting to it. Wake up to this.

Insanity comes from mal-adaptation to the larger system not something inside of us happening.

What is the mal-adaptation? Listening to them, taking it on, mimicking the debauched/sick throng.

FRENEMY TRAITOR

What is the mal-adaptation to the school system who says anything goes? Becoming most low.

Evil is rampant roaming thru the earth seeing who to devour. Warning: be careful every day/hour.

People are psychos, really gotta watch em. Don't let em in they'll do you in. It's who they are/in sin.

It's the contagion of lunacy: in adapting to the crazy maid we actually need her approval, hey

You betrayed my trust. Once you got the upper hand you took my stuff.

Social? Our life is important too, in solitude.

Once the anger is gone (realizing it wasn't right) you come into the light, everything's outa sight.

After 33 years desert wilderness I learned solitude in nature then moved to my new paradise.

Look out the window and ideas come up. Be tracked by a movie in a groove and I'm blocked.

It's not that I don't wanna be with you I just wanna be alone.

Strong work ethic shoots outa bed and works all day. The lazy just wants to hangout and waste.

We adapt to problems by becoming blind to em and that's where the trouble starts so fire em.

They're either good or evil so tell the truth/don't be angry. They'll either wake up or run away.

FRENEMY TRAITOR

Just think you'll be 40, 50, 60, 70, 80 then eternity with a brand new body.

Humans only examine their core delusions after an unbelievable amount of suffering. Stefan Molyneux

Wrong, fruitless or selfish decisions brought God's wrath--an ungentle goading, I remember that.

This is how it works, count on it. How do I know? I went thru it.

A seared conscience loses discernment between right/wrong, good/evil.

Biggest reason to forgive (and not just for lent): we become what we resent.

You are not only responsible for what you say but what you didn't say. Martin Luther

If you hate someone it could be petty competitive strivings that keep you from benefitting/loving em.

If you love em (kids and pets) they'll all get along together too.

It's demon possession they can't help what they do but nip it in the bud or you'll be dead too.

It wasn't you it was the devil but still you gotta get strong so he can't use you.

Stop feeling remorse/embarrassment over past cuz it was satan but now you're free/life's a gas.

Satan made you do absurd, ridiculous and evil things cuz your weakness made you his plaything.

FRENEMY TRAITOR

It's demon possession, they can't help what they do but nip it in the bud or you'll be dead too.

The thing a little demon wants to do is gain your trust but not thru right action but wrongfulness.

For success disentrench from the system cuz it tracks your thoughts and you don't need em.

It wasn't you it was the devil but reinforced by this generation (debauched) it became a knot.

Just step into new life. It's crossing the Great Divide from the angry past to freedom from strife.

Step UP, rise above all problems. Fly above it like a bird looking down on these anachronisms.

Enjoy success, you deserve it. You worked, overcame, matured and walked away from it.

Never adapt to interruptions. You must now manage your time where they NEVER determine it.

Words connected thru meaning AND sound. That's the rhyme, it's higher than paragraphs long.

You shoulda watched what you said to me, and you thinking I was just like you! What an insult, fool.

They didn't hate you it was the devil in you so just repent and it mentally disappears from view.

If everyone hates you it's cuz you're a jerk so just repent then start your work.

FRENEMY TRAITOR

No matter how good they look it's an illusion of Satan and it's ugly inside/take it in stride.

Listen Rustler just cuz you got away with it doesn't mean we're gonna forget it, believe this.

I'm real nice 'til I'm not so don't get me mad or watch out. American citizen

The children of God are your new family and the blood ties are no more, really. No tears, please.

Sometimes you'd like to see em again but how interesting: there's just nothing there to work on.

Satan makes you remember the bad. It helps to know it was a demon and never recalled by God.

Satan wants you filled with embarrassment, remorse, shame over a past faux pas/don't give in.

Love your neighbor as yourself, do what is front of you to do and then you will have a good life.

They become no more important than strangers on the street and after all your tears that's so neat.

Once they see you don't think like them they go out and tell everyone cuz that's just evil humans.

Once your cross the Great Divide blood ties mean nothing and the spiritual ties everything.

Everyone's into "family" and it's a laugh, really.

FRENEMY TRAITOR

Out of many I had ONE family member with spiritual connection surrounding the Savior.

My ONE family member brought me to a whole new life while the others just kept me in strife.

When they're not children of God (born again) they're not family anymore/free of that.

In the twinkling of an eye you have nothing in common with her/him and that's how God does it.

When they're not children of God (born again) they're not family anymore and we're free of em.

Jesus came to divide us, don't forget that. Whoever tells you it's to unite us is a liberalized heretic.

You can't ever be at their mercy or they'll impose stuff on you and it's smelly so always stay free.

In the twinkling of an eye you have nothing in common with him/her--that's how God does it sir.

You don't move in with em/burn all your bridges or let them move in without dates of riddance.

People are sinners, utterly depraved. But through Jesus we have God so repent and be saved.

Children of alcoholics are adapting to the devil. Alcohol is a conduit to him and it's awful.

FRENEMY TRAITOR

No one wants to see their own depravity but weakness allows demons to work it thru us, see.

Humble yourself, pray, seek His face, depart from your wicked ways: God heals you *and* your land.

Thank you God for exposing, tearing down and replanting.

It's the divide and conquer lying spirits that prevail in this age, it's called the Strong Delusion.

Lord expose the whole choir of evil doers and remove them for our future.

It's easy for the world to seduce your kids when they see you as hypocrites.

Our predestined groove can only be found thru repentance, or miss the boat and stay a nuisance.

God is really comin' thru you now you're getting ready to show/make the dough cuz you know.

That's right: One night of sin and your whole life changes overnight.

Being gone so long they see you as enemy.

Should feel secure in our territory. Reason your dog knows he's home for life: he trusts you, silly.

God put it in you: a SEED. Let it grow, design and nurture it--who knows where it's gonna lead?

RECAP. How to succeed greatly: humble yourself, pray, seek His face, turn from wicked ways.

FRENEMY TRAITOR

Your talents should be as simple as a bird singing. It's holy spirit ease: naturally, effortlessly.

Not just your talents but your team is predestined. That gives me a good feeling, not free-willin'.

LEARN TO SAY: "She did this to get back at me" Always see everything as a device then stay free.

Good-looking and glib smiling preachers are successful because they're one with the devil.

Tho' we'll always be sinners, gotta repent of the major ones (holding you down) or you're a goner.

Forgive (overcome obstruction). Become your first nature again, the sweet child people were lovin'.

We're not to respect and include the sinner but withdraw, restrain, draw lines, be an overcomer.

Cat's aren't independent, hon'--they get mad if you're gone too long.

Forgive yourself for anger cuz you couldn't help the demon blowing up, an archetype growing up.

Puritans restrained unhealthy tangents like porn because they wanted to stay high with God.

If you love your child teach em to be likable to others too then all life is happy, loving and cool.

No other religion gives solution to man's fallen state of abomination but Christ and it's simple.

FRENEMY TRAITOR

If you don't have place for something don't keep it but many homes are storage bins/trash pits.

Don't knock, don't come up the stairs, don't bother me. Protect my privacy not make me crazy.

No other religion gives solution to man's fallen state into abomination but Christ/it's simple man.

Common sense comes from God not man.

We're waking up and dumb is getting smart. An evident change: in brain-dead there's a spark!

You're my friend if you love America, Trump, freedom, God & If you hate these things you're out.

The unit is household not neighborhood. Don't spread out (social) but focus therein, that's good.

If you love God you're my sister and if you're my sister and don't love God you're not. Rot.

Jesus said don't even go to the funeral if they didn't love God like you do.

God is all that matters so if you don't love Him blood ties are irrelevant, meaningless, shattered.

Know thyself in this spiritual battle: Do you do good/refrain from evil?

God takes the spirit of anger from us when we realize the reason we were, and it's an oasis.

FRENEMY TRAITOR

Don't feel bad about the times you went off the deep end for it's like a trance, you were lit/in a fit.

Forgive yourself it was just a spirit in you. When we get weak it comes in/destroys more than a few.

You answer a call in them like an echo and suddenly you're in fame kiddo.

Creative process: I know it's God when it starts and I know it's God when it stops thank goodness.

They change things all of a sudden like the monkey's on Chance's Island.

Monkeys learned from apes across the sea--sudden and telepathic. In humans: decent vs. barbaric.

Forgive yourself for when the devil was in ya. You got weak then he did his business thru ya.

Either I'm skiing, or it's chaos. Tanner Hall

I don't have to explain it I just resonate with it.

I hate computers cuz it reminds me of school. C.R. Johnson, Pro Skier throwing trix off mts for big bux.

There's nothing done that hasn't been done before. Don't take it seriously since you've repented dear.

Anything that tracks the mind is not satisfying. You wanna increase inner amplitude by opening.

FRENEMY TRAITOR

It's culture or sexual licentiousness, can't have both. Culture (like reputation) can vanish like smoke.

Every insane thing I did was from society's input. Left to my own I woulda been ok from head to foot.

God said I don't remember you doing it and I didn't see it cuz I erased it through My Son I sent.

I suffered all my life from rejection for being conservative but didn't know that was why it was.

Weak in character just slide into the gutter if that's the narrative cuz they know no better.

Established writer is elegant all day but ultra comfortable cuz it's constant having something to say.

Don't even sprinkle it once in a while with F-talk. Never or they'll peg you and career will stall.

If they don't support your work they're in opposition/will undermine it so drop blockheads/twits.

He called my freeski movie corny and I said hey if they can do that they've a right to be.

Give em a little so it all seeps in then tomorrow teach em again.

You're not alone and forsaken but under God's wing, hidden.

Shake it loose: do everything differently than you've been doing and you will see.

FRENEMY TRAITOR

Get ready to die. That means to appreciate this day maximally and transcend all ties.

Prepare for death tho' it may be decades off. This keeps you from useless tangents/those who scoff.

Oh well, just forget it all and look out the window. You've got a locked gate so they can't get to you.

If you're a writer you write and if a painter you paint. Stop saying what you are if in reality you ain't.

I don't know why God chose me to be a vessel for a Creative Act but it's a real miracle in fact.

Ph.D. in Streets: Depths of hell seeing horrible things and people so now that you know, be sweet.

Think of how long you've carried this burden then see the power and efficiency of forgiveness.

Don't embrace complexity thinking you serve the world. Make it simple to remove the curse.

Just one day without news or anything else online--now I'm rid of the blues and feeling so fine!

Always return to music as your default setting and soon you will branch to the right thing.

Just work then wait.

Impatience is the biggest problem, let God in, give Him time for the final day of victory/success.

FRENEMY TRAITOR

A rising tide raises all boats but a sinking tide sinks em all too just look at Venezuela you fools.

I have felt like the underdog *helpless* as the foreign invasion goes on without cessation.

It's a mentality where virtue signaling reigns supreme cuz no one wants to be out of mainstream.

For success disentrench from the system cuz it tracks your thoughts and you don't need em.

It helps so much to know it was a demon cuz then there's no need for explainin' just forget him.

She's not a backstabber it's the spirit within her but you still gotta cut her lose or bye bye future.

You're in a new life and will never look back. Locked into a new dimension like white from black.

Your art isn't about politics it's about your generation's narrative of such--old slogans outa touch.

The left are sick freaks--we know that--but violently want open borders to totally wreck us.

We win on the war of ideas, they're so false they must rely on crybabies and bicycle locks.

700,000 homeless American kids and left won't lift a finger to help. Democrats, remove yourself.

Is that a strong women yelling like a hyena? Making demands and trying to fool ya?

FRENEMY TRAITOR

Forgive (overcome obstruction). Become your first nature again, the sweet child people were lovin'.

I see what you're up against. A wild, foolish, gullible, group-driven little witch who's also a snitch.

Forgive yourself, it was the influence of other people. You were just too weak and in came evil.

The democrats love immigration due to false compassion and the desire to win elections.

Equal playing field tolerates buffoons.

The nasty EU stands for "tolerance, diversity and human rights" and we are rejecting them all.

Sweeter they are the more virtue signaling but God wants us bold/strong not such obvious faking.

Step UP, rise above all problems. Fly above it like a bird looking down on those anachronisms

EU heads the richest on earth but wants you poor so they make even more as immigration soars.

The new maid is humble and causes no trouble, the other one ran rampant telling all to the rabble.

Sin destroys decades of your life and if He's given you up to it you'll have no control/filled with strife.

In a post-Christian era female goddess religions emerge and lesbians become preachers.

FRENEMY TRAITOR

 **GRIT the best determiner of life success: conscientiousness, dedication, tenacity, get er dun.**

Decades of laborious failed attempts and embarrassing lessons then lift-off with God's blessin'

Your work is perfect tho' you aren't.

You can't teach an old dog new tricks so it took this to break thru the blockhead to bliss.

You could be a foulmouthed floozie for decades and didn't know it cuz it was a demon from Hades.

It was all demons and Jesus erases everything that occurred therein.

The churches have become wimped to adapt to the wimps in the pew who don't want the truth.

We're all sinners--we get caught up in things--but the point is repent then God and angels forget it.

"Low neuroticism" means freedom from negative emotions.

Relax, it was all a demon workin' thru you hon' and it's gone, irrelevant, non-applicable, NONE.

It's good them thinkin' you're dying then they'll leave you alone.

Although people cause trouble or joy, they still come and go so just seek God and on Him rely.

Stop resenting actors God created to teach you things. You learned em, they're gone: evil beings.

FRENEMY TRAITOR

Evil is limitless, so horror opens you up to the dark abyss--a horrible pit you should wanna miss.

Lesson bringing wisdom and success: If you act right you'll be blessed/if you don't life's a mess.

I have often regretted my speech, never my silence. Xenocrates

Due to what Jesus did the past is literally erased and what a blessing and miracle on this day.

We get so high that old problems pale into insignificance--we've gone way beyond them since.

Justice, completion, victory.

Prepare to die, be a child--free of the phony/contrived and frantic deadlines, now be mild.

They get power over you thru intimidation, so if you have no fear (like Trump) how can they win?

I forgive you but can't see you cuz you're evil and it sears my soul.

Ingrown: just wanna be alone! Lock me in my room and throw away the key--that's the happiest place for me.

Don't plan your day just fall into the predetermined groove laid out for you (you still choose).

Oh well, just forget it all and look out the window. You've got a locked gate so they can't get to you.

Jesus came to divide families not to unite them, although it would be nice if they came along.

FRENEMY TRAITOR

How to be heroic: refuse to go along with current narrative and state the truth to the barbaric.

Relish the opportunity to be an outsider cuz it's outsiders who change the world. Donald Trump

It's not really me it's God comin' thru. It's just what I do.

Treat the word "impossible" as nothing more than motivation. Donald Trump

Don't work today just savor and appreciate how far you've come and know you're almost done!

Don't rush to finish forcing the fit but wait to start so it completes itself so it's divinely perfect.

There's no lukewarm with God--He loves or He hates. We're told to hate sin so ok if you're that way.

People/generations die then there's no memory of you anyway so forget em and just be happy.

I hate most books. Long boring paragraphs not all inclusive short sentences which is all it took.

Genius has the capacity to say things simply, not a bunch of words to veil his lack of certainty.

People tend to repeat themselves, gesticulate, go too slow or bore us with unnecessary trivia.

Don't rush the end, completion itself is divine and patience (slow and steady) makes it fine.

Completion of Creative Act: a giant elaborate ceremony of inspiration and success so don't rush it.

FRENEMY TRAITOR

Altho' IQ generally goes down with age for some it goes up- -the *Sage*.

It's not a matter of how much you've done just that *your time has come*.

Era of completion is here, I'm an inch away. But patience says: go easy, go slow, let God has His way.

It's so exciting to know God will complete everything you started. It's His thing, your co-Creator.

I'm waiting for that click in head to start the end. I haven't heard that click yet. Paul Newman

You mean you're so insignificant you don't warrant a platform? No, God has plans, get ready to go.

A book is a book--not like a building where you can see it but every page must be checked, darn it.

Make the books available--publish yourself--then totally rely on God to be your marketer/best sell.

I'm not here to sell books but to do what God told me to. It's my calling, that settles the issue.

One can never know when he will be done until that moment he's done. Thank you Albert Einstein

Just do what you do and suddenly be done.

You're done it's just a matter of *correct and firm* and you've won.

I know you're in a rush to finish but slow down a bit, you need the right frame of mind to be lit.

FRENEMY TRAITOR

You're at your most powerful cuz you're most focused and that's cuz you're elders, confess it.

Your will not mine be done. You lead the way to complete and total world victory, then I've won.

The biggest failures come from finishing too soon. Wait for breakthrough but keep on low like stew.

Sure it's underground but there'll come a point where it all explodes and finally you're noticed.

They shake you up/censure by blocking "likes". Don't be bothered, keep posting, don't think twice.

A long succession of worthless accomplishments or one big creative act that took decades in fact?

They don't care if it took forty years they just think you're old. Transcend this generation/be bold.

There are no grey areas, it's black or white. Go by the book, wishy-washiness is a blight.

Don't worry cuz when the time comes to start you won't be able to not-start, pulled to the end.

Like a string in a sweater that unravels completely that's completion, then you are free.

Don't worry when it's time to start it's like a tidal wave completing itself naturally, so wait!

How to write. Lock em out, look out window, open mind.

Stop cowering. You're made in the image of God--strong, powerful--that's when He's behind it all.

FRENEMY TRAITOR

You're in a new life and will never look back. Locked into a new dimension like white from black.

I feel like a rocket ready to take off.

Plant grows underground then suddenly sprouts--it is seen--and that's exactly how you will be.

Planted the seed then you waited--the biggest part of the journey--before God now rewards it.

I'm savoring the End of the Creative Act, like ocean going thru my veins/correct and firm, FIN.

Completion/retirement is like falling outa structure: our self-imposed urgent deadlines.

Celebrate your total world success tho' you're not done yet the final's locked into place, eh?

I know you want completion more than anything but don't rush the end--let God come in.

Here's the gist: God put talents in you for a specific job so hone those skills, give your twist.

World success transcends the weather, the place, current events or anything else: it's the ACE.

Success feels like an ocean going thru your veins.

You've done the work now relax and live off the fruits.

Prepare for world fame. Success overnight = renowned cuz you overcame all/fought the good fight.

Hippy

Main liberal shove-down: we're all equal, *ONE*.

The liberals you know are still ticked Trump's the boss and will never get over it/accept their loss.

Never accept someone's pronouns: that's the next level of insanity we must adapt to now.

Our president is beloved around the world so you're making fools of yourselves boys and girls.

Trump is a proud man: proud of himself, his achievements and his family--that's a good thing dummy.

Liberal cities are tolerant, politically correct, diversified and covered in needles, trash and feces.

They can't separate out the utopian image from what it *really* is--until it hits em in the face/DISSED.

Collectively mentally ill and there is no bottom to their evil, the contagion of madness in the people.

There's nothing they won't do, these kids. No more lines, like ISIS.

When states turn blue you have massive homeless problems too.

Liberal means you trash your city, allow anything goes, have sanctuary cities/ok citizen murder.

FRENEMY TRAITOR

Things got dirty in the 70's--we see debauched grandmommies justifying everything like trannies.

Political correctness is the mind virus of the left.

Just to be hip do you say bad things? Remember that to us clear minds, it's so embarrassing.

Distressed: It's astonishing to see just how much opposition there is from the anti-rational left.

It's brutal out here trying to get a message across facing brutality, de-platforming, banning.

The horrible names they call us to get the feral mob to attack us and to think it's CNN fake news.

To think that in my free country I can only move around with body guards protected from lib hordes.

Liberals move in mobs while conservatives are just themselves.

Since the liberal mob assembles (to do you in) you MUST have bodyguards, it's just astonishing.

If you really respect multi-opinions it should be no problem that we express em--but it is, isn't it.

People are offended by everything so why does it even matter save our free speech in tatters?

Donald Trump is the most pro-black president we've ever known. Darrell Scott

He's very direct, not like politicians going around and around in circles, all talk. Melania Trump

FRENEMY TRAITOR

Liberals turn on a dime--flipping 180 in an hour, you know something else changed their mind.

If we give in to those taking offense soon we say nothing and less.

If it's an answer they don't like it's a "rant"

They monitor things "on behalf of the audience", how ridiculous with ramifications monstrous.

So the monitor censors in deference to the whole audience? It's tyrannical and I'm not having it.

"I'm asking you to be more respectful" means: curb your talk to what we want or be called awful.

Just censor the smut.

Open inquiry is basis of greatest civilization since best conclusions come after hearing ALL ideas.

Lauren Southern: How tenured hippies ruined everything.

Just cuz they live in their mother's basement, dependent, doesn't make em less dangerous.

California cares more about destigmatizing AIDs than they do about not spreading it/hate.

I'll never get over my fear of those boys—tho' now in their fifties it's seared in my history.

They hate normal people since normies wouldn't be into all their weird crap.

One thing about war: you demonize your enemy.

FRENEMY TRAITOR

According to the crazy left enforcing federal law is the exact same thing as slavery.

The problem is old white people, they say. We just don't get their vision with hell to pay.

Not one scientist agrees you can determine your own gender just by saying so.

We're sick of catering to your trigger warning race/gender BS or safe spaces.

From their vantage point you're old but they're rude so don't go back/be happy/stay bold dude.

The saints said these people are crude and silly, so much superfluity.

If there's one sign of hope, it's this: ingratitude is the howl of hubris, and hubris comes before the fall. anonymous

Censorship FB/Twitter: You can't face your accusers, know why, nor prove them wrong--bummer.

Millennials more concerned with how they'll be viewed than with accuracy of their statements.

We don't wanna live in violent dysfunctional s**tholes infested by black and latin gang members.

Quitting Trump is their new platform--it isn't politics anymore it's the world's dumbest religion.

They wanna remove my only defense/protection not blame the shooters, the reason we need guns.

CNN represents the death of logic. CNN

Antifa-like resistance to all SCOTUS pix.

FRENEMY TRAITOR

Liberal towns are quiet since everyone's afraid to speak but accepted narratives are ok to preach.

Signs to quit your school: Words like equity, diversity, inclusivity, white privilege, systemic racism.

They're not being educated but indoctrinated.

Contract is the basis of civilization for predictability in all our affairs but not to liberals, I declare.

Left is angry Tommy Robinson got out--the far right neo Nazi or whatever else they call the patriot.

Even smart men are a bit jealous of Trump from intrinsic envy of his SMV (sexual market value).

Academically suspect, ideologically possessed.

It's exhausting/debilitating to be in a cold-hearted relationship with those calling you a racist.

What Trump is doing for America is phenomenal and to that degree to liberals he's horrible.

The left is protected for everything it does. It's convinced everyone it's not the enemy, but it is.

Since self-restraint (saying NO) is a strength that's why weak men get into pornography I think.

Trump has radically expanded scholarships to minorities but the dems can't stand these victories.

Tolerance and universal love leads to acceptance of the occult.

Luciferian doctrine: tolerance, accept everything.

FRENEMY TRAITOR

2009: 60% of churchgoers voted for liberals. In other words, the baby killing and LGTB agendas.

You can't hate blacks but it's perfectly ok (politically correct) to hate whites.

Tolerance: "Do what thou wilt" is the whole law.

I believe in sin and can see how a church would be popular if it didn't.

They love Bianci's church cuz it won't mention sin just "inclusion"--same old slide into delusion.

Blacks fail from family breakdown/immorality but it's always called racism, that's their reality.

The mob is dumb and vain. Stefan Molyneux

They hate him so much you know he's for real.

Everything is relative, truth is nonexistent, utopia's within our reach: that is what they teach.

Why should utopians be happier than Christians? We have Almighty protecting, they have nothing.

There's nothing like telling truth to democrats and watching them go nuts. Jesse Lee Peterson

In the past, American blacks went to church on Sunday and dad was in the home disciplining.

Al Sharpton and Obama managed to divide the races more than anyone in the history of America.

You don't love your kids sending them to public schools or new scouts intending to destroy good.

GLOBALISLAM

Unholy Alliance: the Liberals Love 'Em

LOBALISLAM AND MASS IMMIGRATION
KIDS KNOW NOTHING ABOUT PRIVACY/PROPERTY
FACE IT: PEOPLE HATE US CUZ THEY'RE JEALOUS
FOR VICTORIOUS INVASION, START WITH CONFUSION
DON'T STOP THE INVASION OR YOU'RE MEAN TO KIDS
BLACKS: THIS IS YOUR LAND!
LAWLESS LIBERALS DON'T SEE LEGAL FROM ILLEGAL
FROM COMMUNAL TO TOTAL SOLITUDE
THINK OF YOUR PETS--THE THIRD WORLD IS INDIFFERENT!
MODERN DEMOCRACIES COMMITTED TO DIVERSITY
THE COMMUNIST IS JUST A VILLAIN
FREEDOM STATE MEANS CRIMINAL SANCTUARY
ECONOMIC WARFARE: MAKE EM POOR, TAKE CONTROL
OPEN-BORDERS CORTEZ DISGUST
FREE OF GOVERNMENT WE'RE HOMOGENEOUS
WHITES TOO PARALYZED TO RESIST
"ILLEGAL PERMANENT RESIDENTS"
ISLAM LINKS WITH GREENS AND COMMUNISTS
WISH TO SURVIVE, NOT NOT-OFFEND
DON'T INVADE AND <u>DO</u> FENCE ME IN
WATCH WHO YOU TAKE IN
THE PROFESSOR SOUNDS LIKE A FOOL
NON-WHITE NATIONS BLOCK IMMIGRATION
COMMUNIST TERMS: CITIZENS OF THE ECONOMY
KALERGI PLAN OF MASS IMMIGRATION
GLOBALISTS WANT BLIND CONSUMERS WITHOUT ROOTS
DIVERSITY IS CRUELTY
IT'S NOT YOUR GUESTS--OPEN BORDERS IS THE GIST.
BREXIT: THE BRITS TOTALLY AGAINST THIS!
LOVE YOUR WHITE RACE, BE CALLED "RACIST"
AND TO THINK IT'S THE CHURCHES!
DESPICABLE TRAITORS
HOSTILE GROUPS ENSURE MIGRANT BENEFITS
FLYING THE FLAG MEANS WE'RE RACIST
WE DON'T WANT 'EM HERE
REPLACISM IS SADISM

GLOBALISLAM

Unholy Alliance: the Liberals Love 'Em

If you haven't been invaded in your home you don't see the savagery of open borders. It's 21st century warfare and America's under attack: Weaponize the third world and flood/get us back. Why do kids think it's OK to invite ALL their friends to your house? No respect for your INDEPENDENCE. What does your independence demand? it's about property, *privacy*, silence which they don't understand. Whites are already a minority and some are hated by their own family. Who is causing this racist trouble? White liberals who hate whites even more than invaders might.

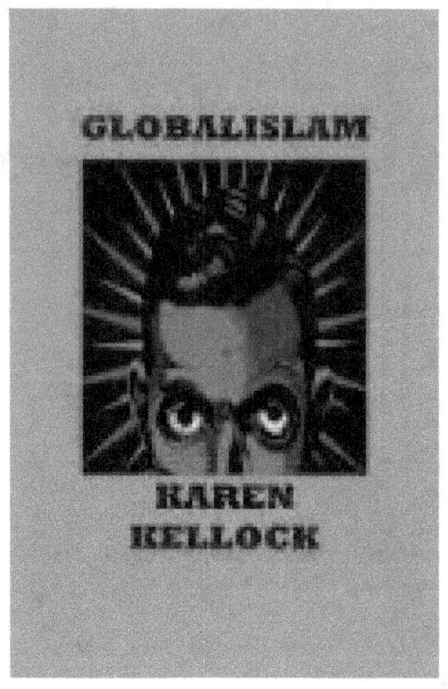

GLOBALISLAM

Unholy Alliance: the Liberals Love 'Em

GLOBALISLAM AND MASS IMMIGRATION

If you haven't been invaded in your home you don't realize the murderous savagery of open borders.

It's called the Ontologically Fatal Insight: that reality was NOT what you thought--a psychotic shock.

Just like Europe, they trash the place. Food/clothes so kindly donated--strewn about, what a disgrace.

The globalist's plan is to use weaponized third world populations to take over the planet and we hate it.

It's 21st century warfare and America's under attack. Weaponize the third world and flood/get us back.

Remember our equation: High boundaries plus high order = DISGUST.

Invaded by gang of uninvited boys and cops wouldn't help me. The boys knew it but ROs gave remedy.

KIDS KNOW NOTHING ABOUT PRIVACY/PROPERTY

Why do kids think it's OK to invite ALL their friends to your house? No respect for your independence.

What does your INDEPENDENCE demand? it's about property, privacy, silence which they don't understand.

Honduras: If you don't stop caravan/take these people back I'm cutting all foreign aid to you: fact. Trump

Soros is behind the sexualization of children, open borders, Muslim flood of refugees and protestors, see?

GLOBALISLAM

Open borders people have no sense of what it's like to be invaded but it's a quick way to learn.

White man is already a minority in his own country and every day hated more even by his own family.

Who is causing this racist trouble? The white liberals who hate whites even more than POC's might.

Time to stop illegals from getting taxpayer dollars. They're experts at gaming our system over and over.

African American unemployment is lowest it's been in recorded history but still they say Trump brings misery.

Every time an illegal alien votes it cancels out the vote of a U.S. citizen, making us a minority: WARNING!

Trudeau's budget is completely focused on equity. Not on dangerous floods of immigrants you see.

FACE IT: PEOPLE HATE US CUZ THEY'RE JEALOUS

There are people who hate us so much that it's either their way or they will destroy it. Abraham Lincoln

If you think people like Hillary Clinton should impose their will by brute force, vote damrat. If not, vote rep.

The democrat's answer to misery is more open borders, sanctuary cities and to abolish ICE: YIKES!

Democrats are the agents of mayhem.

Whites are unique in the way they pay respect to the people they defeat.

SAD STATS: They proliferate fast, we don't. They want a brown universal dumbed down de-gunned race.

Biggest cramdown since kindergarten is "we're all one". Don't you dare say I'm one with them: scum.

GLOBALISLAM

Geo Soros said he would ban all conservatives to stop the collapse of world gov by calling us "rage and hate".

There's a worldwide backlash against globalization and its secular aristocracy who are mean and filthy.

They've used the number "11 MIL. illegal immigrants in America" for 27 years but it's ten times that sir.

This is not an invasion with guns and tanks but a VOTING BLOCK invasion and Americans are enraged.

Third World voting block invasion means one thing: The UN is in control and America is not sovereign.

We are witnessing a giant UN army smashing borders and sovereignty, worse than Europe's tragedy.

They brought in ten million Muslims to Europe and red-carpeted them everything for free, now this.

FOR VICTORIOUS INVASION, START WITH CONFUSION

The same creeps telling your boy he's a girl is behind this invasion: the left wants America's destruction.

The giant army from the south is marching in to seize the wealth of the north as the new (reverse) colonizers.

Third world civilian invasion is nothing but a weapon system of the democrats who will do anything.

It's a UNITED NATIONS INVASION of North America with the southern borders completely smashed.

United Nations has officially invaded Mexico with a marching army of tens of thousands which will grow.

It's nothing but a UN army waving it's flags with the FRONT of little girls and babies not military grunts.

GLOBALISLAM

The ultra-rich uses communism and third world populations as their ARMY. All over the world/so alarming.

As the invasion breaks into America the left is ready and waiting to radicalize em as a new block of voters.

NATIONAL EMERGENCY: UN LAUNCHES INVASION OF UNITED STATES USING MIGRANT CARAVAN

In Ellis Island you were quarantined for six months to make sure no diseases, can you believe this?

How the UN operates (you should know): with giant masses of starving people under their control.

Venezuela collapsed, causing a chain reaction sending seven Latin American nations into El Norte.

Government wants more people on food stamps/welfare so now they're pouring in, what a crisis friends.

Hours of footage of city gates blown off and barbarian hordes pouring into Rome, our falling home.

DON'T STOP THE INVASION OR YOU'RE MEAN TO KIDS

As our nation's overrun with it, democrats say: "Don't stop anybody or you're mean to little kids".

We're invaded, we've been trained to accept this and now they're collapsing the third world into the U.S.

The democratic party voter registration drive is happening right now as the hordes of illegals show.

In Europe they bring in fifty thousand at a time and put em in villages which become literal HELL.

There are 6 billion people collapsing and the U.N.'s gonna use it--America's reaction must be drastic.

GLOBALISLAM

Flying the flag of another country as you push in/break into another country is one thing only: INVASION.

If we're not prepared to stop this caravan, how big will the next one be and how many more in weeks?

Mobs vs. jobs: These are devastating images of hordes breaking through border fences, dear God!

If they'd been let in, another billion in increasingly larger and more expectant (PRESUMPTUOUS) groups.

The UN is a corrupt organization and globalist engine. They planned this just like the European invasion.

Immigration destroying Europe/threatening America. Gorgeous Europe--gone forever, trash everywhere.

People who don't share our values are coming to suck the country dry.

The democrats don't care about illegal aliens they just want the vote for personal power and wealth!

These Illegals bring in crime because they don't have our values and America will be another S-hole.

BLACKS: THIS IS YOUR LAND!

Blacks: This is your land. Wake up/act like it--let no more illegals in this country cuz they hate you man.

What about whites strung out on drugs cuz they've been pushed out/lost pride/guilt from being white?

Our very justified WHITE PRIDE has been stolen by those wanting us outa their way--recall how Obama lied!

We're living through an orchestrated invasion! Groups this size don't mobilize without funds/organization.

GLOBALISLAM

George Soros Open Society Foundation funds liberal lawyers to block getting the foreigners outa here!

These aliens impose their will and bring their friggin' flags into our country? This can't be happening.

We are drowning in illegal aliens. If Trump can't do something immediately he's no friend.

LAWLESS LIBERALS DON'T SEE LEGAL FROM ILLEGAL

Liberals don't see the difference between **LEGAL** and illegal immigrants because they are **LAWLESS**.

It's a giant public relations stunt (to upset old order) and the way they do it is put women/children in front.

Who's behind it? Catholic charities need new bodies and voters are needed in the democratic party.

The world is now a dangerous/violent place so if you're not willing to fight for what you have you'll lose it.

Violence surging in this country due to the violent people coming into this country but you don't believe me?

Left insanity includes open borders, America is racist, white privilege and POCs are morally superior.

80% of the caravan are men under 35.

There is no reason to back governments who are going to create this pressure on our southern border!

Strapping young men in new clothing with women pushing five children in a stroller in front of them.

Illegal immigrants are coming to take black's jobs. Blacks, please **WAKE UP--** they hate your guts!

GLOBALISLAM

It's not politics, it's the devil looking to institute one world government and God doesn't want this done.

It's not invasion but contrived attempt to collapse the last sovereign nation, the world follows, then ONE.

God loves nations and variety. He doesn't want ONE BIG BLOB so the conflict is over that: devil vs. God.

FROM COMMUNAL TO TOTAL SOLITUDE

I even grew to hate housekeepers in my house. Any incursion of a different reality was too much!

I grew to hate housekeeper day. I made plans to escape it somehow, everyone get outa my way!

I don't want ANYONE in my house! That's my personal sanctuary and you smell or maybe it's what I sense!

And after going through all that, I know about home invasion and having to put up with stuff you hate.

Always borrowing things--get the heck out, stay out, get your own, GTH, never come back, sink in swill!

Sending these people back will be the biggest mass effort we've ever seen from any president in history.

ALL Americans care about is immigration, immigration, immigration! We want out home back/rid of em.

A giant and delicious backlash against elitist billionaires who want us drowning in foreigners.

Isn't it strange thousands of people simultaneously decided to march north just before our elections?

It's one thing to help people, it's another thing to SHOWER them with goodies for breaking the law.

GLOBALISLAM

Polls show more Americans want ZERO immigration not the established levels because we're sick of it.

Stop having babies to save resources but then import half the third world to make up for it.

Liberals have proven illegal aliens are more important than citizens or our children who need help.

All white people just have to die. Oprah Winfrey

The white man freed the slaves--and lost life and limbs to do it--but still they are always blamed.

Buckle up folks, somethin' huge is comin'

THINK OF YOUR PETS--THE THIRD WORLD IS INDIFFERENT!

We love our pets--cats and dogs--but these third world pops hate em or neglect em, it's bad man.

What would happen if millions of foreigners marched into Pakistan? Maybe now you can understand.

Using child separation to open us up/destroy our borders--not a word re: children of prisoners.

Left hates Trump cuz they hate prosperity. They want us all poor/dumbed down to accept tyranny.

Whites are the most accepting/tolerant in the world. No other race accepts floods of foreigners.

Whites went from tolerance to weakness, afraid to stand up to invasion, abuse and meanness.

We Americans are very nice till we're not--we're quickly reaching that point so buddy watch out.

Why on earth would you let all these strangers into your house? The whole world's laughing at us.

GLOBALISLAM

Real men would be lined up on the border, not let em in to suck off the public trough/intruders.

Told not to discriminate whites don't prefer their race over another but it's very different all over.

At first they're too ashamed to be a patriot. But later when it's accepted they joyfully do it.

Classic Trump: equilibrium disruption, resolution. Drop bomb then say "I love Theresa Mae".

Making em adapt to us is like we're "superior" cuz all races are alike says the liberal (inferior).

CNN and all fake news is globalist and that's why they hate America-first president, a nationalist.

Need Muslim ban or we've had it man.

MODERN DEMOCRACIES COMMITTED TO DIVERSITY

Modern democracies are committed to diversity but then things don't work and we're all unhappy.

Despite nation's average IQ there are those who shoot through higher/not offended or angered.

Increasingly nations are defending unique culture and traditions against this globalist hegemon.

To MAGA we gotta spread it to the world by being on the side of nationalism for all, forever.

As Obama was a closer to globalist disaster Trump is ENDING the secular One World Order.

Why we love him, the modern day Sansom: he's the Great White Hope saving all the nations.

GLOBALISLAM

Trump: Immigration is politically destabilizing the entire country in this national emergency.

They're bringing the mess, the s-hole societies, to our country. Donald Trump

If you love your nation/race you argue against diversity and I've already explained this travesty.

If someone calls you a bigot turn off the spigot or never see em again, the idiots.

CNN globalists want us taken over and destroyed.

White people usually have only tiny families now, no match for a thousand cousins all around.

Every culture's different in set up. Things like interpersonal distance, reaction time, frame ups.

Let's not talk about labels just the free stuff I'm going to give everyone. Alexandria Cortez

Socialists are always bread and circus free stuff then take everything you have and more you nut.

THE COMMUNIST IS JUST A VILLAIN

He's a communist but really just a villain.

Mad Mother Merkel guaranteed there would be NO LIMITS on money migrants entering Germany.

Whites went from tolerance to weakness, afraid to stand up to invasion, abuse and meanness.

Seven acid attacks a day in London and we know where that came from but can't say it or prison.

They have an agenda: dispossessing those of white European descent from their birthright.

GLOBALISLAM

It's how they treat dogs and cats too--everything is strange, harsh, brutish.

Stop pushing white guilt and making white students feel less than others.

Multiculturalism and diversity are just anti-white policies.

Christianity is about mercy not the harsh punishments of the East.

The new groups flooding in will have an edge due to their nepotism, identitarianism and tribalism.

"We don't want all these people here" said everyone all throughout Europe to Soro's deaf ears.

Our piece of the pie is much smaller or we'll be banished altogether and you want open borders?

When country becomes prosperous they wanna take your money to buy groups, so stay on top of it.

Listen to the race hustler who runs away, always blaming it on slavery not the absent family.

It's unreported, understand that! You don't know the extent black on white slaughter/it's a fact.

FREEDOM STATE MEANS CRIMINAL SANCTUARY

Freedom State means sanctuary state.

As whites we gotta be forted against Muslims but also blacks out to get us if we love Trump/facts.

Non-whites aren't having anti-your-people propaganda pushed on em so they can be proud.

For the entire border little children are used as subway tokens to get into America/fraud, scam.

POC's (people of color) are knockin' em out (whites all over) and it's unreported (study deeper).

GLOBALISLAM

Pedophilia in migrant camps: It's when you keep the kids together with adults that this happens.

Cortez wants to eliminate ICE and the protector of your sovereignty, the constitution--yikes.

Shrieking liberals are advocating burning ICE down and several offices are under siege now.

Ms. cortez wants to ban guns and open the borders completely: prepare for mass slaughter lady.

Well paid globalist pawns: Late night comics don't have talent like Johnny Carson, come on.

Anyone for open borders hates blacks, whites, women, kids and pets.

Taught stupidity and feelings are all that matters so 40% of kids want socialism like Sanders.

Is it jealousy re: income inequality? Seeking to make the rich poor not the poor to have more.

ECONOMIC WARFARE: MAKE EM POOR, TAKE CONTROL

Economic warfare makes countries poor to control em, tho' globalists dying it's still happening.

Socialists will fight you for the crumbs on your table so it's all about "free stuff" not these labels.

Extremist open border democrats make me sick cuz they don't think of us putting up with this.

White South Africans can't live on their own soil but blacks can claim all of Europe, that's all.

If Europe doesn't welcome millions of impoverished low IQ men in, it will be ruined. EU saying

GLOBALISLAM

99% of the inventions that we take for granted were by white men, that hunted/targeted vermin.

They want news taken down cuz for most of us the idea of being replaced is too much to fathom.

They are majority minority cities.

What a great thing, our cities are flooded with CEOs, doctors, lawyers and other immigrants.

As long as the new majority conforms to us it will be fine, but we know that won't happen anytime.

More ethnic diversity = more conflict and segregation.

A black is 20x, an Hispanic 8x more likely to attack a white than visa versa but this info is censored.

Americanism not globalism is our credo. What we want is victory for the world. Donald Trump

Everywhere we look border walls are going up, not coming down. Celebrate nationalism.

Democrats are going for hyper-globalist open borders just when the world is rejecting this horror.

OPEN-BORDERS CORTEZ DISGUST

Ms. open-borders Cortez is triggering such a swing to the right, HA HA it's happening overnight.

Our value system stands 100% opposed to everything they stand for so they don't assimilate ever.

Demographic path to liberal control of USA.

Democrats don't care about children, illegal or American. Jesse Lee Peterson

GLOBALISLAM

It's a false outrage, folks. They don't care about children (look at all the abortions) but votes.

Masochism is also the communist spirit. Not only take mine but give away gifts from ancestors.

We have nothing in common except we're both human beings. Every thing they curse, I believe.

You and I are split, poles apart--nothing whatsoever in common, for a start.

Elite Plan: Make culture deteriorate to be controllable.

Like the Fabian socialists they slowly develop the new mind and it's hell on earth, cruel/unkind.

College gives right attitude towards minorities and means to live as far away as possible. Jared Taylor

Self-righteous politicians chant mantra of integration while living in gated communities/protection.

Not an ounce of sympathy for whites being displaced by non-whites seen as bigots, a blight.

"Integration is our goal" but not for me or my children. --Most politicians

A cobweb of watch groups needed for diversity-maintenance--cuz it's unnatural and we hate it.

FREE OF GOVERNMENT WE'RE HOMOGENEOUS

Free of government, communities are racially homogeneous: churches, families, clubs, happiness.

Nothing could be more obvious: diversity of tribe/religion means violence, hatred and derision.

It's not just school brainwash cramdown it's also the inset cosmology "we are all one" insanity.

GLOBALISLAM

Why isn't diversity good for Mexico? You mean they wouldn't want to be reduced to minorities so low?

Could Mexico be tricked to think it's "cultural enrichment" if we took over their country/government?

Mexicans are more clever than wimpy whites—they'd recognize an invasion of their rights.

Racial Diversity is a one-way issue. Only whites are expected to give what is theirs to you.

Ultimate insult: demand whites celebrate diversity—their capitulation, lost influence and country.

Whites built successful desirable societies and desperate non-whites want badly to live in them.

We demand Mexico open their borders, let us buy land and vote down there just like they do here.

Multiracialism is a suicidal fad and elite globalist set-up that's bad: we've been had.

WHITES TOO PARALYZED TO RESIST

In the face of dispossession whites are too paralyzed to resist so they succumb.

Race Realism is so simple and so obvious: the races vary in temperament and intelligence.

It's not racism to not want your grandkid black or when the neighborhood changes to move: fact.

Different outcomes due to different abilities not prejudice but in America they're taught to hate us.

Kids should be taught about race in the fifth grade but they're taught it doesn't exist instead.

GLOBALISLAM

If we live in two different worlds psychologically there's no way we can share a space physically.

We are the first civilization in history to give up what is ours then search for a place to go, darn.

Whites are giving up what was theirs and marching off the stage of history: unprecedented, truly.

Self-destructive insanity (of whites being displaced from their country) is new to our species.

Blacks commit a disproportionate amount of crime (statistics from Dept. of Justice and FBI).

They WANT blacks and whites fighting so they can make new laws and take control instantly.

Racism has never existed but is being used to incite riots, take control and kill resistance.

Thousands of whites killed by blacks every day but police investigate the "N" word on Le Bron's gate.

Instead of being angry at crazy kids just see they bought the whole scam and ALL of it's points.

Illegal aliens now named "illegal permanent residents"

"ILLEGAL PERMANENT RESIDENTS"

Illegals are destroying black community with jobs, crime and health care but liberals don't care.

Since 1965 USA has seen the largest invasion in human history: 61 million is a CATASTROPHE.

The alt-right is against one group dominating another so this mass immigration is a fetter.

GLOBALISLAM

The Alt-Right are just race realists (of the obvious) but are always called white supremacists.

Lead you into sin so we all fall down then they take control of everything around.

The Luciferian spirit is anti-God, anti-Christ and anti-you and it's goal is complete and total control.

He/she is demon possessed to ever push an agenda like that

New cause with electoral prospects: illegal aliens while American poor people get lip service.

Globalists' plan: Islamify the entire world.

Demographics is destiny and oh what a tragedy.

In nations or homes, prosperity is followed by decadence as walls come down/inflow of immigrants.

Obama said rural towns were "too white" so brought in third world pops to vote/dominate overnight.

Greece prohibits protests against having your town invaded/trashed in collusion with Islamofascists.

"Riots, vehicular attacks, priest beheadings or honor killings aren't linked to migration" -Macron/dumb

France, Germany: 80% migrants are on the dole. Deport them or it's suicide from dysfunctional souls.

ISLAM LINKS WITH GREENS AND COMMUNISTS

Islam linking with green and communist movements to vote everyone's rights away despite disparity.

World War III begins with demographic leftist globalist directives voting all our rights away.

GLOBALISLAM

Macron/Merkel take marching orders from same source of course, not just dumb creating the worst.

They're dominating/raping women everywhere and the police do nothing in Paris, Berlin, London.

It's always been the same: kill the men and rape/enslave the women and that's what's happening.

The crusades were a defense against multi-century Islamic invasions of Europe.

Their goal was to conquer Europe and was being achieved then they fought back, a defensive war.

They celebrate this history and say that's the goal: take over again.

They took away your culture. Without a culture you're intimidated and submit to their tyranny.

Whites are blamed for slavery when they ended it and all cultures had slaves/blacks most of it.

European castles: the defense against Muslim slaveholders until quite recently in history.

For whites self-defense has become an impractical art of social/economic suicide. Stefan Molyneux

WISH TO SURVIVE, NOT NOT-OFFEND

When the fear to offend outweighs the fear to survive you can say to the western world: bye bye

Mass rape of conquering armies of old is what we are witnessing in Germany and Sweden today.

They don't understand those failed states are the way they are because of the people who live there.

GLOBALISLAM

No concept of morality outside the west--you take what you can as long as benefits outweigh costs.

Europe is a dusty collection of dead empires and new arrivals are the maggots on it's corpse. Black Pigeon

Who the hell is Merkel to decide what are German values? Certainly not this but she's not budging.

Who is Merkel to decide what are German values? Certainly not this but she won't budge ya know.

Who knew globalism meant communism, open borders, hostile invasion and abolishing culture?

True: Illegal immigration has decimated black communities but the media never talks about this.

"All cultures are alike" abandons all ideals of architecture, math, beauty--it's sophistry/malarkey.

Sheer depth and richness of texture in arts and sciences meant the west had no equal in the world.

DON'T INVADE AND <u>DO</u> FENCE ME IN

See this: As a couple you're all alone in nature then someone moves in next door--joy no more!

The righteous sees evil that's coming and gets out the way, the evil say "what the heck, it'll be ok".

20 years in desert solitude then moved into country neighborhood and wow, have to build a wall.

Two kinds of elites: lions relying on strength and moral character vs. foxes who win by cunning.

Emigrate, colonize, then "what happened?" when it's too late and we wake up in a foreign country.

GLOBALISLAM

The biggest racism today is white-on-white racism. Stefan Molyneux

Guilt cultures stabilize society but always lose with attack cultures who never feel guilty.

They give you the impression whites are attacking blacks to make them look like the victims.

When outcomes of blacks vs. whites don't turn out same we blame whites not genetic differences.

Affirmative action is: gaining advantage at the expense of others.

Mexico accepted money from the U.S. government for that territory so their moral claim is silly.

They don't come here cuz they love Thomas Jefferson but for the money, called "quality of life".

They're here for cold economic reasons and have no loyalty to the United States.

The problem is black inability not white oppression. Jared Taylor

Yes Asians have a higher IQ but no conformist nation can ever produce a scientific revolution.

The white race is a sinking ship but this can still be turned around--just start speaking, it's legit.

I don't get triggered anymore cuz I don't have people around who trigger me--walls made me free.

WATCH WHO YOU TAKE IN

Watch who you take in. Stop the hippie commune thing it's wrecking everything. These are spirits, see?

You like nice things so they all want to live with you, see? But third parties are your end--be free.

GLOBALISLAM

See Color of Crime. Shootings: blacks 31x and Hispanics 12x more likely than whites to murder.

We will burn Europe to the ground. Tayyip Erdoğan

Migrant violence and terror is "Europe's fault, not linked to mass immigration". Macron

For every black attacked by a white, twelve whites are attacked by blacks and that's a fact.

Whites are the first people in history to be gladly dispossessed of honor, land, country.

Whites are the first people in history to gladly say: "sure, take my land, diminish my power."

Since whites have sub-replacement fertility their only answer is polygamy or extinct by 2050.

Diversity is not our strength as lost uniqueness means blobs. Race realism is true and we hate mobs.

Whites deferred gratification and restrained fierceness and thus they built the European castles.

Low IQ pops go right on the dole and you think that's good stuff well then you and I are done.

It's not fat but the speed of collecting water. It's released in a moment, removing the fetter.

No society survives once diversity is introduced but we have to: coming unglued/ugly feuds.

With forced diversity instead of loving the strangers with time it leads to hate/see em as slime.

THE PROFESSOR SOUNDS LIKE A FOOL

He may be a professor but sounds like a fool.

GLOBALISLAM

It's not whites holding blacks back but illegal aliens taking the jobs but they won't face that.

Blacks have a weird affinity to illegals when the latter take away their jobs, housing and hospitals.

By coming here illegally they are all criminals and because of that they need to be deported.

A striking reverse association between population density and happiness: wide open spaces = bliss.

Nothing could help blacks more than a wall and deportations. But liberals hate all that, corrupted.

Islam uses demography/migration as tools of asymmetric warfare yet elite dictum is: have no care!

What makes it different is these upsets are scripturally prescribed, approved and mandated.

Let's be kind to them so they be kind to us when a majority: good luck on that false reality.

If I had to be under a slaveowner let him be white. Jared Taylor

Survival depends on wall (total control) and Muslim Ban (violent ideology vs. founding principals).

Elitism: Islam is nice/tolerant and the west has been nasty to it; land isn't ours but whoever wants it.

A spectacular double-standard: what is taken for granted by out-groups is denied to whites, pooh.

NON-WHITE NATIONS BLOCK IMMIGRATION

NO non-white nation would ever let in mass immigration. It's preposterous to think of it even.

GLOBALISLAM

Every other group can organize along racial lines--only whites bring reaction, what's going on?

Poisonous anti-white atmosphere of universities: "my group is nothing to be proud of" tragedy.

In this era of crazed anti-racial discrimination they would ban whites due to skin color? Yah sir

Staggering hypocrisy, spectacular injustice as whites diminish into complete disappearance.

Pathological altruism (letting em all in) is a soft form of cultural suicide. Stefan Molyneux

Race realism vs. new age: racial differences 100% environmental otherwise everyone's equal.

Race realism vs. new age: race differences 100% environmental otherwise everyone's equal.

Socialism: philosophy of failure, creed of ignorance, gospel of envy, equal sharing of misery. Churchill

Born dumb, stay dumb. Born smart, stay smart--minus a few points lost due to trauma.

NEW Italy gets more police/prisons as it clears illegal "gypsy" settlements in towns/cities.

COMMUNIST TERMS: CITIZENS OF THE ECONOMY

Jerry Brown's "citizens of the economy" means us being cogs in the wheel of global capitalism.

It's common knowledge today but in the 80's they locked up and drugged people thinking like this.

If you said globalist Builderbergers in the 70's it was mandatory drugging for sure but now it's clear.

GLOBALISLAM

Every other group can organize along racial lines but not us? Please explain this.

Causes of mass immigration are cleverly concealed by elites but falsely portrayed as inevitable.

KALERGI PLAN OF MASS IMMIGRATION

Kalergi: Future world citizens a new mixed breed resulting from mass immigration/miscegenation.

Kalergi: Europeans interbreed with non-whites/Asians for a brown pop without identity/easily controlled.

Kalergi: Ethnic separatist movements combined with mass migration = way to destroy the nations.

Kalergi: In order for Europe to be controlled by an elite there must be a homogeneous mixed breed.

Thinking Europeans should fold tradition into one mixed race promotes policies for minority interests.

Merkel won prestigious prize of Kalergi Foundation for excellence promoting this criminal plan.

Multiculturalism: weakened disparate population without national, historical or cultural cohesion.

Kalergi plan is used by governments intent on genocide of European pops thru mass immigration.

UN: Limit births and promote mixed marriages creating a single world race directed by a central authority.

As Europeans are made the renounce their origins they're to welcome the brown "children of Kalergi"

Kalergi Plan advanced stage: Fusion of Europe with Third World.

GLOBALISTS WANT BLIND CONSUMERS WITHOUT ROOTS

GLOBALISLAM

The globalists want blind consumers so tell us give up traditions/identity as humanitarians of the world.

European integration amounts to genocide so not telling em is national suicide.

As they prioritize those skipping the line they make legit immigrants wait longer, that's Canada.

For me this diversity crap started at fifteen and overnight life went mean.

When whites won't speak against enemy (fear of being called "racist") they bring out the worst.

Attacking people for things they didn't do by how they look: you're on board with it, I'm not.

Queen hates modernity and I don't blame her cuz it's false theories pursuant to globalist misery.

Multiculturalism is a modern political ideology which is used as a battering ram sanctioning a tragedy.

Opposing the myth, multiculturalism doesn't bring prosperity but poverty and lack of trust/enemies.

We need zero-pop for them not us, we need polygamy or we'll go extinct before century is up.

Only way of fighting back is by excluding Islam from the West hermetically and permanently.

Diversity means: Forcing us to live with people we're not compatible with--it's empty and mean.

Forcing people on us is great cruelty. God's wrath is: being suddenly surrounded by strangers.

God's wrath is: natural disasters or being suddenly surrounded by strangers.

DIVERSITY IS CRUELTY

GLOBALISLAM

See how cruel diversity is to stop it. Problem is gradually adapting to it then suddenly waking to it.

Inside humans is robotic circuitry of aversion to diversity, a survival device of great value today.

No diversity around red mountains today but I fear Islamic invasion since it's polygamy-friendly.

Gotta think of these things, implications are profound and psychosis-producing to the crowd.

I did my thing: I moved and got a fence and locked gate. Better do it soon or I pity your fate.

Can't stem the tide it's overwhelming glad I'm dying.

Worst torture: people forced on you for a moment or more.

Globalist mindset imposed thru schools always sells it as cool and it's picked up by fools.

It's so bad they're leaving their country to flee it in order to come here and make you submit to it.

Don't go to France if you can't speak Arabic.

Royal wedding not a celebration of British values but multiculturalism, Marxism, black liberation.

IT'S NOT YOUR GUESTS--OPEN BORDERS IS THE GIST.

Stop complaining about your guests and blame open borders instead.

7 billion people and most are retarded by design--this explains your trouble keeping friends.

They'll do anything to find racism to justify vastly different outcomes when it's all IQ you bums.

GLOBALISLAM

Whites: The reason you are demonized constantly is cuz they want what you have desperately.

It's all OUR fault they are bad. There is no other explanation for it the school authorities said.

Globalists are an anti-human anti-free speech religion and they even call it that in documents.

What a sadistic plan: being demoted by crowds of brutal rapacious strangers is hell man.

First they get rid of other religions then align with Islam cuz it's authoritarian: that's the plan.

Tommy Robinson has been disappeared and they're told to not report it. UK is evil/Theresa Mae

UK put an order out that no one's allowed to talk about it. This is Soviet style tyranny folks.

REVOLUTION: Demonstrators storm the UK government, sick of the torment

The government of the UK is an outside globalist force. Brexit: attempt to get gov back on course.

This is the beginning of the second world revolution against the globalists, Jacobins and parasites.

Humanity will no longer be manipulated by Bezos wanting to bring millions in, weaponized against us.

BREXIT: THE BRITS TOTALLY AGAINST THIS!

Just like when Hitler bombed the Brits thinking they'd roll over. The Brits always turnover.

Brits were 65% against war until Hitler bombed then they were 85% FOR: watch what happens now.

Half of all Americans live in sanctuaries protecting immigrants.

GLOBALISLAM

Instead of extreme discernment resulting in merriment you let them all in from a failed experiment.

Ireland has referendum on lowering birthrate but no country can vote on their third world immigrants?

No nation can vote against toxic third world onslaught but they can to kill babies--globalist plot?

You can have feminist-inspired abortion or demographically flourishing population but not both.

Choose: mass immigration or pro-life sentiments. There is no other option even nationalism.

Ireland has just made it's own contribution to Europe's descent into a secular globalist abyss.

Though only 10% pop, Muslims vote as a block so people get into power and we're forsook.

Nationalist populism is fueled by pervasive and deep anti-elite sentiment: we're sick of em.

LOVE YOUR WHITE RACE, BE CALLED "RACIST"

Any positive representation of white people's history, culture or capabilities is inherently "racist".

Achievements of non-whites are transformed into collective accomplishments of that race.

The media's goal is that whites have no part in mass culture at all.

Marxists want open borders--they despise Christian culture and know barbarians would crush her.

Now we know why they're here--to be voters--how do we get rid of em faster?

Reasoning: Muslims would never do this so they didn't do this and if they did they're not Muslims.

GLOBALISLAM

Systemic racism/unconscious bias: that's all we hear when before it was all ok with them and us.

When everyone does better, civilization/prosperity. But the globalists want us to live under austerity.

Focus on Islam removes the heat from those orchestrating it all but soon it'll be totally outa control.

Italy is giving us hope. New coalition is planning to dump half mil migrants--they're like Trump.

Migrants in Italy are getting leery as new gov encroaches to either deport them or pull their money.

Save the nation! Far-right Italian parties plot array of sweeping curbs on asylum/immigration.

They're gonna get em: Landlord confrontation/new centers of detention ready for deportation.

Imams registered with state, unauthorized mosques closed and no new ones--shut that gate.

People are waking/rising up against the managed decline of Europe and those letting her fall.

AND TO THINK IT'S THE CHURCHES!

And to think it's the churches investing in open borders--like the Lutheran council making a bundle.

It hurts feeling a stranger in a strange land but when it's your home it's a real disaster happening.

They're coming in like a flood. Stop the churches Trump cuz they're the investors making a lump.

So the churches are traitors flooding us with strangers? That's amazing when you think about it.

GLOBALISLAM

What if deacon came to your home and opened the door to thugs? There is no difference--need Trump

Churches think they're being Christian by flooding us with strangers. Virtue signaling = dangerous.

In the UK they say "run, hide, tell" to the ancestors of World War II, what hell.

I was invaded by thugs of both genders over several decades and I say open borders is Hades.

They destroy all that is precious to you. It's no different than an rapacious army marching through.

Animals are tearing up the beautiful European countrysides, the little villages history describes.

Everything you hold dear they think nothing of destroying cuz it's a totally different tribe I fear.

Lutheran Council is one traitor selling us out for cash. Each migrant brings a price once processed.

There is no end to appeasement.

They are completely different from us--opposed diametrically, genetically and culturally

DESPICABLE TRAITORS

Despicable traitors brought in an invading army for votes and money.

Millions of hostile invaders flooding into the land.

You must throw off the guilt the elites have been programming and tormenting you with.

By letting in low IQ pops--the dumb--they'll go along with anything, nation of controlled bums.

GLOBALISLAM

Germans the smartest scientists and musicians or revert to the total opposite, Merkel's non-logic

Genocide need not be a mass slaughter but just telling em not to breed while nourishing others.

White genocide: encouraging abortion then bring in those with 20 children and support all of em.

Long term plan: Replace uppity whites by telling em to abort then bring in high-fertility alien pops.

It is so evil, well-thought out, disgusting, criminal, unheard of, beyond shocking: 100 year planning.

Genocide isn't always violent, just Impose measures intended to limit births within a group.

Genocide doesn't have to be concentration camps, rounding people up, or execution. Just a decision.

Genocide: flood country with invaders hostile to indigenous peoples or founders of that nation.

Take over government then let in a swamping wave of foreigners to aggressively colonize that nation.

HOSTILE GROUPS ENSURE MIGRANT BENEFITS

A hostile group uses the state power to ensure migrants get benefits, housing, medical and cash.

Government gives em the benefits to breed rapidly once settled in our homeland/fat and happy.

Mass immigration is not accidental but by design.

In the hearts of Europe's peoples is an ancient fear of loss of homeland to Islamic invaders.

GLOBALISLAM

YAY: Soro's audacious attempt to install a pro-EU technocrat as Italy's Prime Minister has failed.

There's a big difference between being welcoming and giving strangers the keys to your house.

They pretend to be conservatives or even nationalists but suddenly you see they sure aren't it.

Whatever the people want they get the opposite and what politicians want the people reject.

Elites live in gated communities with armed guards so don't mind the floods of strangers in mobs.

They lie to the people, spend all time virtue signaling and have pure contempt for the native pop.

Dear Scots: Your leaders don't care about you--they're just importing votes/signaling virtue.

The implications of their policies or the fact they'd even consider them is enough: ban em.

E-Race White: That's why the globalists push abortion--white genocide.

Anti-bullying means anti-Islamaphobia.
Libs see nationalism as silly tribalism we shoulda outgrown by now.

Now flying our flag means we are intolerant of immigrants or just flat-out racist.

FLYING THE FLAG MEANS WE'RE RACIST

Socialism is poison and a poisonous idea is destruction.

The decline of the west is so into the latter stages we no longer have the will to fight savages.

To destroy/displace a culture you need psychology, mainstream media and institutional support.

GLOBALISLAM

Elites want a despondent pathology displacing the nationalistic and optimistic Europeans.

The special quality of group's defended territory is insulation from demographic disturbance.

A group can suffer setbacks but as long as it has it's territorial space it can recover.

Territory ensures survival. Mass immigration diminishes genetic interests of the native pops.

Multicultural surrender = pathological, pro-white against displacement = adaptive/rational.

The more I have land (my territory) and a fence then demographic changes effect me less.

A free society requires high IQ populations, and there is not one low IQ pop on earth that is free.

Immigration is a government program and immigrants are here for the subsidies in general.

Building first world economies pulls up the third world, lowering first world to be equal does not.

WE DON'T WANT 'EM HERE

Is there any doubt in Planet X or do we now have two suns? The gravitic effects are the earth's hex.

Globalism is coming to an end in Europe along with the whole notion of multiculturalism.

With globalization the host nation must accommodate the immigrants: the backlash is now, thanks!

It's a strange era when bad reputation marks good character, victimized by the worst on earth.

GLOBALISLAM

A secular globalist world can only exist by attacking the religious values of our traditions/past.

Emancipatory politics: power of the state used to disentrench us from our traditions/roots.

Globalism sees traditional roots as constraints to our true selves or is that just what they say?

Justice, equality and liberty in a globalized society: What a total mess that turned out to be.

Give me your tired, your poor and those who want a free WIFI connection. Michelle Malkin

Although IQ is stable one can still degrade through sin, association or being disabled.

REPLACISM IS SADISM

Biggest reason for population replacement immigration: white guilt, western ethnomasochism.

Replacism: Interchangeability, the false idea you can replace anything and it will be the same.

Replacism: False idea of the insignificance and irrelevance of the thing being replaced, like us.

High taxes de-incentivizes Europeans from births and incentivizes immigrants to come to the west.

Trump will put a tariff on Canadian cars and they'll make em here. He's so smart, a genius/seer.

How hegemonies keep their empire: keep everyone off balance adversaries and allies alike.

Champagne socialists push diversity to please the youth while not having to live with the poop.

GLOBALISLAM

Throwing acid in one's face with goal of disfigurement is a foreign and barbaric practice.

As London becomes less British it has a higher crime rate/more badness.

Einstein was a xenophobe just like me. He hated strange, brutish foreign customs and freaks.

Democrats ruin every city they run cuz they're globalists: debauched and evil not homespun.

Merkel is facing mutiny over her mad, dangerous open door migration policy.

Merkel madness is about to topple and I'm so glad she's been murderously awful for her people.

How does evil Soros get his political gain? My overseeing Europe's "managed decline".

Throwing Tommy Robinson into prison population is like throwing a baby to the shark's ocean.

Military is trained for zombie patrol cuz they know huge hordes of people will be outa control.

UN has said global pandemic is the only savior of world government seen as the solution.

Our country's not for everyone, you must give back to it.

If whites don't start having many babies America will be a third world s--t hole country.

THE HERD IN WORDS
HIX POLITIX
HOW THEY RUINED US
JUST SKIP DINNER
LE FEMME AND THE COMMUNIST SPIRIT
LIBERAL CHAOS & ROT
LIBERAL DOUBLETHINK
LIBERAL GALL 1 & 2
LIBERAL SHOVE-DOWNS
LOCK YOUR GATE
MANUAL FOR SUPERIOR MEN
MODERN ART FROM HELL
MOSTLY FAKE
NOTES TO CHAMPS 1 & 2
OVERCOME FRENEMIES
PC MAKES US CRAZY
PEOPLE ARE CRUEL
PEOPLE PROBLEMS 1 & 2
PERSECUTED GENIUIS
POLI-PSYCH MYSTERIES
PRETENTIOUS SLOBS
QUEEN BEE
RETURNING TO FIRST NATURE
THE SCHOOLS SCREWED EM UP
SEASON OF TREASON
SEPARATE MEANS HOLY
SOCIAL HYPNOTISM
SOLITUDE SOLUTION
SUPERCILIOUS
TOAD TO PRINCE
TRIALS CYCLES
TRUMP VS. GROUP
TRUST IN TRASH
THE TRUTH ABOUT PEOPLE
UNDERHEANDEDLY CLEVER
WALK TALL WITHIN WALLS
WE'RE NOT ALL ONE
WINNERS SKIP DINNER
WORK OR SMERK

AUTHOR BIO

Karen Kellock Ph.D.

Ph.D Political Psychology, UCI 1976
Post-Doctoral: UCI Medical School
Department of Psychiatry
Grants NIMH, NIAAA

Ph.D. dissertation "A Systems-Theoretic View of Pathologic Interaction" made an early mark as the "Wife of the Alcoholic Syndrome". Postdoctoral research at UCI Medical, Dept. of Psychiatry on the systems surrounding pathology on NIMH and NIAAA federal grants: *The Contagion of Madness: The Psychology of Neurotic Interaction and Pathological Systems*. Therapy tool Therapeutic Playwriting introduced the play *Mary and Murv: Gruesome Twosomes in the Alcoholic Marriage*. She taught Abnormal Psychology and Pathological Systems Theory at UC and CSU campuses and developed "the Debris Theory of Disease" in five books and website: (**www.karenkellock.org**): *Champion Guides, Daily Fastarian, Just Skip Dinner, Arts of Paleo Fasting, Ageless Cornucopia. Manual for Superior Men is a* pick-it-up-anywhere book that you can't put down (20,000 Kellockialisms) and ever on your desktop it should be found (or this Ebook for superior wordsearch of new jargon).

www.ingramcontent.com/pod-product-compliance
Lightning Source LLC
Chambersburg PA
CBHW061720250726

48657CB00002B/700